P9-BZO-405

The Sound of L

By Alice K. Flanagan

This is my
left leg.

I can hop on
my left leg.

4

5

6

This is my left arm.

I can mop with my left arm.

9

10

This is my
left hand.

11

I can dig with
my left hand.

13

14

This is my left foot.

I can kick with my left foot.

17

18

This is my left eye.

19

My left eye sees left and right.

21

Word List:

left

leg

Note to Parents and Educators

The books in this series are based on current research, which supports the idea that our brains are pattern-detectors rather than rules-appliers. This means children learn to read easier when they are taught the familiar spelling patterns found in English. As children encounter more complex words, they have greater success in figuring out these words by using the spelling patterns.

Throughout the series, the texts provide the reader with the opportunity to practice and apply knowledge of the sounds in natural language. The books introduce sounds using familiar onsets and *rimes*, or spelling patterns, for reinforcement.

For example, the word *cat* might be used to present the short "a" sound, with the letter *c* being the onset and "_at" being the rime. This approach provides practice and reinforcement of the short "a" sound, as there are many familiar words made with the "_at" rime.

The stories and accompanying photographs in this series are based on time-honored concepts in children's literature: well-written, engaging texts and colorful, high-quality photographs combine to produce books that children want to read again and again.

Dr. Peg Ballard
Minnesota State University, Mankato

childsworld.com

Published by The Child's World®
1980 Lookout Drive • Mankato, MN 56003-1705
800-599-READ • www.childsworld.com

ACKNOWLEDGMENTS
The Child's World®: Mary Swensen, Publishing Director
The Design Lab: Design
Michael Miller: Editing

PHOTO CREDITS
© inxti/Shutterstock.com: 6; Maryna Kulchytska/
Shutterstock.com: 13; Marcos Mesa Sam Wordley/
Shutterstock.com: 17; Pollapat Chirawong/Shutterstock.
com: 10; Samuel Borges Photography/Shutterstock.
com: cover, 18, 21; Sergei Kolesnikov/Shutterstock.com:
2, 5; Valentina Proskurina/Shutterstock.com; 9; wckiw/
Shutterstock.com: 14

Copyright © 2017 by The Child's World®
All rights reserved. No part of this book may be
reproduced or utilized in any form or by any means
without written permission from the publisher.

ISBN 9781503809222
LCCN 2015958490

Printed in the United States of America
Mankato, MN
June, 2016
PA02310

ABOUT THE AUTHOR

Alice K. Flanagan lives with her husband in Chicago, Illinois, and writes books for children and teachers. Ever since she was a young girl, Ms. Flanagan has enjoyed writing. Today, she has more than 70 books published on a wide variety of topics. Some of the books she has written include biographies of U.S. presidents and first ladies; biographies of people working in our neighborhoods; phonics books for beginning readers; informational books about birds; and career education in the classroom.